Sushi for Beginners:

The Best and Easy Sushi Recipes for Home Cook

Copyright 2017 by Ella Porter - All rights reserved.

This document is geared towards providing exact and reliable information regarding the topic and issue covered. The publication is sold on the idea that the publisher is not required to render an accounting, officially permitted, or otherwise, qualified services. If advice is necessary, legal or professional, a practiced individual in the profession should be ordered.

- From a Declaration of Principles which was accepted and approved equally by a Committee of the American Bar Association and a Committee of Publishers and Associations.

In no way is it legal to reproduce, duplicate, or transmit any part of this document in either electronic means or in printed format. Recording of this publication is strictly prohibited and any storage of this document is not allowed unless with written permission from the publisher. All rights reserved.

The information provided herein is stated to be truthful and consistent, in that any liability, in terms of inattention or otherwise, by any usage or abuse of any policies, processes, or directions contained within is the solitary and utter responsibility of the recipient reader. Under no circumstances will any legal responsibility or blame be held against the publisher for any reparation, damages, or monetary loss due to the information herein, either directly or indirectly.

Respective authors own all copyrights not held by the publisher.

The information herein is offered for informational purposes solely, and is universal as so. The presentation of the information is without a contract or any type of guarantee assurance.

The trademarks that are used are without any consent, and the publication of the trademark is without permission or backing by the trademark owner. All trademarks and brands within this book are for clarifying purposes only and are the owned by the owners themselves, not affiliated with this document.

Table of Contents

Book Description

Introduction

Chapter 1. Essential Tools and Ingredients for Sushi Making

Chapter 2 Sushi Sauce and Salad Recipes

Chapter 3 Vegetarian Sushi Recipes

Chapter 4 Fish and Seafood Sushi Recipes

Chapter 5 Meat Sushi Recipes

Chapter 6 Dessert Sushi Recipes

Conclusion

Book Description

Japanese food is rich in culture and sushi is one of the immediately recognizable Japanese cuisine. Sushi is the traditional Japanese way of cooking food that includes serving seasoned rice in a combination of fish, seafood, vegetables, meat, fruits and other ingredients. Sushi is extremely versatile and offers an impressive variety of colorful flavors. The cuisine originated in the East, but today it is extremely popular food in the West. Preparing sushi doesn't require a lot of effort and patience.

With the help of this beginner's sushi making guide, start to make this delicious food at your home today. Often people think making sushi is a delicate art and can't be achieved by amateurs. However, this book will clarify and explain the sushi preparation techniques and make sushi making fun and enjoyable for a beginner like you. The book will show how easy it is to make sushi even for people who are not familiar with Japanese cuisine.

The book offers practical sushi preparation guidance with a friendly voice. With this beginner's sushi guide, enjoy one of the world's healthiest and most palate-pleasing cuisines in the comfort of your own home. Sushi can be an inquired taste for food lovers, so this book gives you a wide variety of sushi recipes including vegetarian, sushi salad, fish, seafood, meat, and even dessert sushi recipes. So why wait, gather some quality sushi grade ingredients, buy a rolling mat, and start to make some sushi.

Introduction

The book is the perfect sushi-making guide for the beginners. Delicious and healthy, sushi is for anyone who loves to eat healthily and enjoy serving special meals to friends and family on special occasions, birthdays or during any family event. This complete book on sushi for beginners provides all the important information you need to get started on sushi making. You only need a few simple tools and sushi grade cooking materials, and you can start making a wide variety of delicious sushi recipes.

Chapter 1. Essential Tools and Ingredients for Sushi Making

Let's discuss the essential tools and equipment's you need to make sushi at your home. Here are 7 essential tools that will help you master sushi:

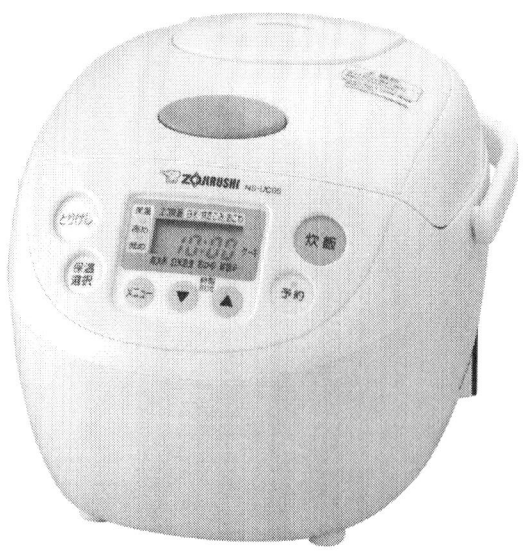

1. A Suihanki: Perfectly cooked rice is an essential element of good sushi. Professional Japanese sushi restaurants use shank or a rice cooker.

2. Hangiri: Once the rice is cooked, you need a bowl to place it, and then add sugar, salt, and vinegar. A wooden container known as hangiri is the best choice.

3. Shamoji: You have to mix the cooked rice with a rice paddle, so excess moisture probate and rice are ideal for

making sushi. Shamoji is ideal when you need to work the rice in the hangiri.

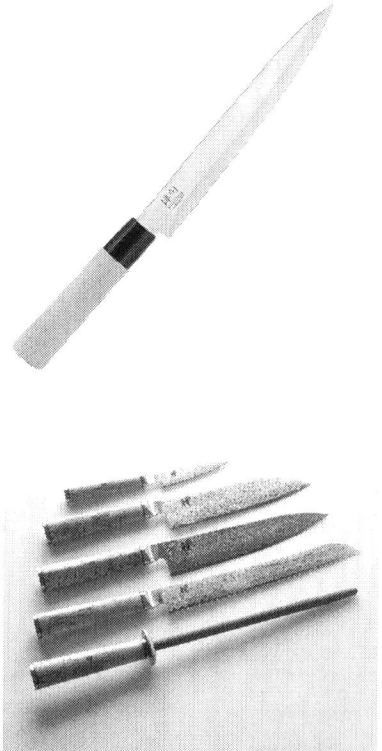

4. The Knife: You need a knife for sushi. It is even better if you own a set of sushi knives. For a beginner sushi maker, the above knife will do.

5. The Sharpening Stone: Your knives need to be sharp for proper sushi cuts. You need a sharping stone like the above to keep your knives sharp.

6. The Makisu: Before cutting them, you need to roll beautiful California and maki rolls. The bamboo mat known as makisu is the tool you need for it.

7. The presentation: To get authenticity to the dish and follow the Japanese sushi tradition, you need these.

We discussed the tools that you need. Now discuss the ingredients that you need:

Sushi Rice (Sushi –Meshi)

Good quality sushi rice is important to make top quality sushi because sushi rice is the foundation of the sushi. You need to choose the best rice, then wash it, soak it and then cook accordingly.

Rice Vinegar (Gomez)

With cooked rice, you need to mix a combination of salt, sugar and rice vinegar to give it that sweet and tart flavor. You can find good quality rice vinegar at Amazon or in your local Japanese grocery store.

Kombu

Kombu is a must ingredient to make the very best sushi rice for your sushi. Kombu gives the rice that hint of dashi flavor. You need to place it in the rice cooker during the rice soaking and cooking period.

Sake

Along with kombu, sake is also important. It also gives the rice a hint of dashi flavor.

Wasabi

You can add wasabi to the dipping soy sauce or place on the surface of the sushi rice. Some people like wasabi with sushi while others hate it. Wasabi is made from green wasabi root and offers a strong flavor.

Soy Sauce (Soya Sauce)

Soy sauce is the core sushi ingredients, and sushi is not complete without it.

Sushi grade fish

What is sushi grade fish is not clearly defended? You can buy sushi grade fish from the local chain grocery store, order online or from your local Japanese store.

Nori

You need good quality sushi nori to make that perfect sushi. Remember, good quality sushi nori is black and avoid buying any green nori.

Sushi Ginger (Gari)

Gari or sushi ginger is usually served with sushi. Gari is meant to eat between dishes or after sushi to help cleanse the pallet. Enjoy your sushi with gari however you like it.

Green Tea (Ocha)

It is a Japanese tradition that green tea is served with sushi. Like sushi ginger, green tea provides a refreshing break between bites.

Sushi Vegetables

Sushi vegetables such as cucumbers are an important element of sushi. Cucumbers are crisp, clean, refreshing and add balance out the flavors.

Chapter 2 Sushi Sauce and Salad Recipes

Now we are going to discuss a list of sushi sauces and then salad recipes

Garlic Mayo

Ingredients:

- Garlic powder – ½ tsp.;
- Ichimi Togarashi – ¼ tsp.;
- Honey – 1 tbsp.;
- Lemon juice – ½ tsp.;
- Kewpie mayonnaise – ¼ cup.

Method:

1. In a bowl, add the ingredients listed ingredients, from top to last. Whisk all the ingredients together and put the sauce into a squeeze bottle.
2. Serve.

Eel Sauce

Ingredients:

- Sugar – 2/3 cup;
- Dashi – 4 tsp.;
- Shoyu – 1 cup;
- Mirin – 1 cup;
- Sake – ½ cup;

- Cornstarch – 1 tbsp.;
- Water – 2 cups.

Method:

1. In a pot, add sake, dashi, sugar, and mirin and place the pot over high heat. Stir until adding the dashi and sugar are dissolved.
2. Once start boiling, add the soy sauce and bring to a boil again, then lower heat and simmer for about 20 minutes.
3. Mix water and cornstarch in a glass.
4. Slowly pour the mixture into the boiling sauce. Stir and mix.
5. Remove the pot from the heat and let it cool. Continue to stir.
6. Once cooled, pour into a sauce bottle.

Yum Yum Sauce

Ingredients:

- Rice wine vinegar – 1.5 tbsp.;
- Mirin – 1.5 tbsp.;
- Melted butter – 1 tbsp.;
- Garlic powder – 1 tsp.;
- Paprika – 1 tsp.;
- Kewpie mayo – 1 cup;
- Cayenne pepper – ½ tsp.;

- Granulated sugar – 1 tsp.;
- Water – ¼ cup.

Method:

1. In a bowl, add melted butter and 1 cup of kewpie mayo.
2. Then add 1 tsp. garlic powder, 1 tsp. paprika and ½ tsp. cayenne pepper, 1 tsp. granulated sugar.
3. Then mix ¼ cup water, rice wine vinegar and mirin and whisk.
4. Pour the sauce into a bottle and keep in the refrigerator overnight.

Sweet Soy Sauce

Ingredients:

- Mirin;
- Shoyu.

Method:

1. To a pan, add 1 cup of soy sauce and 1/3 to ¼ cup of mirin.
2. Bring the sauce to a boil and stir occasionally.
3. Once the mixture reaches boiling point, lower heat to low simmer.
4. Simmer for 10 minutes.

Miso Mayo

Ingredients:

- Hondashi – 1 tsp.;
- Mirin – 2 tbsp.;
- Miso paste – ¼ cup;
- Heavy mayonnaise – 1 ½ cups.

Method:

1. Into a bowl, add 1.5 cups of heavy mayo. Then add ¼ cup of miso paste.
2. Add 2 tbsp. mirin, 1 tsp. hon dashi pellets.
3. Mix until hon dashi pellets have dissolved.
4. Keep in a bottle.

Japanese Ginger Dressing

Ingredients:

- Diced onion – ½ cup;
- Peanut oil – ½ cup;
- Carrot – 1 large;
- Minced fresh ginger root – 3 tbsp.;
- Minced celery – 1 large stalk;
- Rice wine vinegar – 1/3 cup;
- Water – 2 tbsp.;
- Tomato – 1, fresh;
- Soy sauce – 4 tsp.;
- White sugar – 2 tsp.;
- Lemon juice – 2 tsp.;
- Minced garlic – ½ tsp.
- Salt – ½ tsp.;
- Ground black pepper – ¼ tsp.;
- Sesame oil – 1 ½ tbsp.

Method:

1. Chop, dice and mince all your vegetables. Put in a blender and blend.
2. Blend until smooth and creamy.
3. Then pour into a squeeze bottle and keep in the refrigerator for a few hours.
4. Shake before use.

Three Sushi Sauces

Dynamite sauce

Ingredients:

- Sriracha hot sauce – 2+ tbsp.;
- Mayonnaise – ½ cup

Method:

1. In a bowl, whisk until well combined. Keep in the refrigerator until ready to use.

Mango Sauce

Ingredients:

- Rice vinegar – 1/3 cup;
- Sugar – 1/3 cup;
- Salt – 1/3 tsp.;
- Ripe mango – 1 large;

- Vegetable oil – 2 tbsp.

Method:

1. Add salt, sugar, and vinegar in a small saucepan. Over medium heat, bring just to a simmer. Whisk until sugar is dissolved.
2. Chop the mangos, place in a blender with vegetable oil, cooled sugar-vinegar mixture, and blend until very smooth. Keep in the refrigerator.
3. Pour into a sauce bottle and use.

Eel Sauce

Ingredients:

- Mirin – ½ cup;
- White sugar – ½ cup;
- Soy sauce – ½ cup.

Method:

1. In a small saucepan, combine all the ingredients and whisk well.
2. Bring to a boil and then reduce heat to simmer until sauce has reduced to ¾ cup.
3. Remove from heat and keep in the refrigerator.
4. Add in a sauce bottle and serve.

Deconstructed Sushi Salad Recipe

Ingredients:

- Short grain brown rice – 2/3 cup;
- Medium cucumber – 1, cut into thin slices;
- Avocado – 1, pitted and cut into thin slices;
- Shelled edamame – ½ cup;
- Shredded carrot – ½ cup;
- Pickled ginger – 1 ½ cup;
- Smoked salmon 3 ½ ounces, cut into small pieces;
- Sesame seeds – 1 tbsp.;
- Nori – 1 sheet, cut into thin strips;
- Wasabi paste – 1 tsp.;
- Rice vinegar – ¼ cup;
- Soy sauce – 2 tbsp.

Method:

1. Cook the brown rice according to the package directions. When cooked, remove from heat and cool completely.
2. In a large bowl, combine the rice with sesame seeds, smokes salmon, pickled ginger, shredded carrot, edamame, avocado, and cucumber.
3. In a small bowl, whisk soy sauce, rice vinegar, and wasabi.
4. Toss the salad with dressing, add the nori strips on top and serve.

Sushi Rice Salad

Ingredients:

- Japanese style sushi rice – 1 ½ cups;
- Seasoned rice vinegar – ¼ cup;

- Caster sugar – 1 tsp.;
- Nigella seeds – 2 tsp.;
- Frozen podded edamame – 200g, balanced, drained and refreshed;
- Radishes – 4, trimmed and thinly sliced;
- Avocado – 1, chopped;
- Sashimi-grade Salmon – 300g, center-cut, thinly sliced;
- Pickled ginger and coriander leaves to serve.

Dressing:

- Light soy sauce – 1 tbsp.;
- Sweet chili sauce – 1 tbsp.;
- Rice vinegar – 2 tbsp.;
- Wasabi paste – 2 tsp.;
- Olive oil – ¼ cup.

Method:

1. Cook the rice according to package instruction.
2. Meanwhile, in a bowl, combine 1 tsp. salt, nigella seeds, sugar, and vinegar.
3. Stir through the rice and cool on a tray.
4. Combine the dressing ingredients in a bowl. Divide rice among bowls and top with slices of salmon and edamame mixture.
5. Serve garnished with pickled ginger and coriander leaves.

Sushi Salad with Brown Rice, Crab and Avocado

Ingredients:

- Rice vinegar – 1/3 cup, divided;
- Sugar – 1 tbsp.;
- Soy sauce – 1 tbsp.;
- Wasabi paste – 1 to 2 tsp.;
- Sesame oil – 2 tsp.;
- Chunk crab – 2 cabs, drained;
- Carrot – 1 medium, cut into 1-inch pieces;
- English cucumber – 1, quartered wise and thinly sliced;
- Green onions – 3, thinly sliced;
- Drained sliced Japanese pickled ginger – 3 tbsp., chopped;

- Sesame seeds – 1 tbsp.;
- Cooked brown rice -1 ½ cups;
- Ripe avocado – 1 firm;
- Toasted nori – 1 (15 cm), cut into very thin stripes.

Method:

1. In a bowl, whisk together soy sauce, sugar, and 4 tbsp. vinegar until sugar is dissolved.
2. Pour over cooked, cooled rice and toss to mix.
3. Whisk together sesame oil, wasabi, and remaining vinegar and set aside.
4. Add sesame seeds, pickled ginger, onions, cucumber, carrot, and crab to the rice.
5. Drizzle with wasabi mixture and toss.
6. Cut avocado into wedges and add to the salad.
7. Sprinkle with nori strips and serve.

Simple Sushi Salad

Ingredients:

- Sushi rice – 80g;
- Small head of broccoli – ½, cut into florets;
- Handful of kale;
- Avocado – 1 ripe, mashed in its skin;
- Low-salt soy sauce;
- Wasabi paste – 1 tsp.;
- Limes – 2;
- Runny honey – 1 tbsp.;
- Ginger – 1 cm, grated;
- Hot-smoked salmon – 120g;

- Pea shoots – 50g.

Method:

1. Cook the rice according to package instructions.
2. Steam kale and broccoli in a steamer, place on top until rice is just tender.
3. Place the greens and rice in the bowl.
4. In a bowl, add mashed avocado, juice of 1 lime, wasabi paste, and soy sauce.
5. For the dressing, in a jar, pour 1 tbsp. soy sauce. Add the honey and remaining lime juice. Add ginger.
6. Place the salmon over the green and rice and sprinkle the pea shoots on top.
7. Keep the bowl in the refrigerator until ready to serve.
8. Then before serving, shake the dressing and pour over the rice and salmon. Mix and serve with avocado on the side.

Chapter 3 Vegetarian Sushi Recipes

In this chapter, we are going to discuss vegetarian sushi recipes

Beetroot and Green Spelt Sushi

Ingredients:

- Green spelled preparation;
- Green spelled – 200g, washed;
- Water – 400g;
- Rice vinegar – 1 to 2 tbsp.;
- Salt and sugar;

Sushi Filling:

- Nori sheets – 5 to 6;

- Beetroot – 1 to 2 pieces;
- Carrots – 1 to 2 medium;
- Cucumber – 1/3;
- Avocado – ½ to 1;
- Soybean sprouts – 1 hand full;
- Some cress.

Green spelled preparation:

1. In a pot, add the green spelled with water (1:2). Bring to a boil, then lower the heat and boil on low heat for 30 to 40 minutes.
2. Once the green spelled is soft, remove the pan from the stove.
3. Mix the green spelled mass with a pinch of salt, sugar and 2 tbsp. rice vinegar. Let the mixture cool.

Sushi preparation:

1. Prepare the vegetables, cut the garden cress and wash the soybean sprouts.

Making sushi:

1. Place nori sheets on your sushi mat, keep the round side up.
2. Spread the green spelled on it evenly. Leave 2 to 3 cm space on one side and 1 cm space on another.

3. On the green spelled, place the soybean sprouts, cress, cucumber, avocado, beetroot, and carrot. Then roll the nori over it.

4. Make a sushi roll and push it tight.

5. Cut the roll into thin slices and serve with wasabi and soy sauce.

Cucumber Sushi Rolls

Ingredients:

- Cooked Japanese rice – 1 ½ cup;
- English cucumber – 1, cut into quarters, lengthwise, hollowed;
- Vegetable oil – 1 tbsp.;

- Red bell pepper – ½, finely diced;
- Asparagus – 3 stalks, stems picked and finely diced;
- Scallions – 2, finely chopped;
- Button mushrooms – 4, finely chopped;
- Dried seaweed nori – 2 sheets;
- Sriracha sauce – 1 tbsp.;
- Rice vinegar – 1 tbsp.;
- Soy sauce – 1 tbsp.;
- Wasabi and soy sauce for dipping.

Method:

1. Add oil and vegetables in a pan over medium-high heat. Cook until vegetables are cooked but crunchy, about 4 minutes. Remove from heat.
2. Add soy sauce and sriracha sauce and mix well. Now add Japanese rice and mix well.
3. Remove from heat and place rice in a bowl. Add rice vinegar, mix and cool to room temperature.
4. Place the nori on a flat surface. Spread ½-cup rice evenly, roll and wet the edge of the sheet before finishing rolling.
5. Pick up a piece of cucumber, twist and enter the rice wrapped nori into the cucumber hole.
6. Cut both ends with a sharp knife.
7. Slice the cucumber piece into desired thickness.
8. Serve with wasabi and soy sauce.

Quinoa and Vegetable Sushi Rolls:

Ingredients:

- Nori sheets – 4 to 5;
- Quinoa – 1 cup;
- Water – 2 cups;
- Ground ginger – 1 tsp.;
- Sea salt – ¼ tsp.;
- Rice vinegar – 1 tbsp.;
- Agave nectar – 1 tbsp.;
- Avocado – ½;
- Cucumber – ½, medium;
- Baby carrots – ½ cup;
- Baby romaine – 1 cup;

- Low-sodium tamari soy sauce to taste.

Method:

1. To the inner pot of your rice cooker, add ground ginger, salt, water, and quinoa. Close the lid and cook on white rice setting.
2. Once cooked, remove the quinoa from heat and stir in agave nectar and vinegar.
3. Cool the quinoa and sliced cucumber, baby carrots and avocado into the long thin strip.
4. On a bamboo mat, place a nori sheet and place 2/3 cups of quinoa in the middle of the nori sheet.
5. With wet fingers, spread the quinoa into a thin layer.
6. Place a row of baby romaine leaves around the edges.
7. Top with avocado, carrot and cucumber slices.
8. Roll the nori with the bamboo mat.
9. Set sushi roll aside, and repeat with the remaining ingredients.
10. Slice the sushi rolls and serve with tamari soy sauce.

Sweet Potato Sushi Rolls

Ingredients:

- Nori sheets – 6;
- Wild rice mix – 2 cups, uncooked, rinsed and drained;
- Water – 5 cups;
- Rice vinegar – 2 tbsp.;
- Maple syrup – 2 tbsp.;
- Ground cinnamon – 1 tsp.;
- Sweet potatoes – 2 medium, baked;
- Avocado – 1, peeled, pitted and diced;
- Sliced almonds – ¼ cup;
- Reduced sodium tamari sauce to taste.

Method:

1. Place the rice in the rice cooker.
2. Add 5 cups of water and cook on brown rice setting.
3. Transfer cooked rice to a bowl and stir in, cinnamon, maple syrup, and vinegar until well mixed.
4. Allow rice mixture to cool and slice avocado and sweet potatoes into thin strips.
5. On a bamboo mat, place a nori sheet, place 9 spoonfuls of rice on top, and spread with wet fingers.
6. Place a row of sliced sweet potatoes on one edge, top with sliced almonds and avocado.
7. Roll the bamboo mat.
8. Set aside and repeat with the remaining ingredients.
9. Slice and serve with reduced sodium tamari sauce.

Vegetarian Mexican Sushi

Ingredients:

Spanish Rice:

- Olive oil – 1 tbsp.;
- Yellow onion – ½, finely diced;
- Short-grain brown rice – 2 cups;
- Garlic – 2 cloves, minced;
- Vegetable broth – 2 cups;
- Water – 1 cup;
- Unsalted tomato sauce – 1 (14 ounce) can;
- Canned green chilis – 2 tbsp.;
- Ground cumin – 1 tbsp.;
- Tomato paste – 2 tbsp.;
- Fresh chopped cilantro – ½ cup;
- Fresh lime juice – 2 tbsp.;
- Salt and pepper to taste;

No-cook walnut taco meat:

- Walnuts – 2 cups;
- Sun-dried tomatoes – ¼ cup;
- Liquid amino – 2 tbsp.;
- Ground cumin – 1 tsp.;
- Ancho chili powder – 1 tsp.;
- Smoked paprika – ½ tsp.;
- Liquid smoke – ½ tsp.;
- Cayenne pepper a few dashes;
- Black pepper to taste.

Sushi rolls:

- Nori – 6 sheets;
- Avocado – 1, pitted and sliced;
- Bell pepper – 1, thinly sliced.

Method:

1. In a large shallow saucepan, heat the olive oil over medium heat. Add the onion and sauté until translucent. Add the garlic and rice and sauté for a few minutes.
2. Add the cumin, green chilis, tomato sauce, water and broth and bring to a boil. One boiling, lower the heat and simmer on low heat, covered. Once the liquid has been absorbed, and rice is tender, stir in salt, pepper, lime juice, cilantro and tomato paste. Transfer to a bowl and cool to room temperature.
3. Meanwhile, make the taco meat. In a food processor, combine all the taco meat ingredients and pulse until begins to clump together. Transfer to a bowl and set aside.
4. With plastic wrap, wrap a bamboo sushi-rolling mat. On the rolling mat, lay out a sheet of nori paper and spread ¾-cup rice evenly onto the nori paper with wet hands.
5. On one edge of the nori paper, make a taco meat line, top with avocado and bell pepper.
6. Roll the nori paper tightly and slice with a sharp knife into sushi slices.

Chapter 4 Fish and Seafood Sushi Recipes

Salmon Roll

Ingredient:

- Seasoned Sushi rice – 1 cup;
- Makisu;
- Wild Alaskan King Salmon – ½ lb.;
- Nori – 5 half-sheets;
- Bowl of water.

Method:

1. Once the sushi rice is cooked, season with 4 part vinegar, 2 parts sugar and 1 part salt and cool.
2. Place a handful of rice on the rough side of the nori.
3. With your fingers spread the rice and make a shallow line in the middle of the rice bed.
4. Make 1 cm thick rectangular pieces of salmon and place the slices on the line.

5. Wet your fingers and roll the nori sheet. Slice the nori sheet into pieces and serve.

California Sushi Roll

Ingredients:

- Sushi rice – 2/3 cup;
- Nori sheet – 1;
- Surimi – 6 sticks;
- Avocado – ½.

You can also add:

- Masago;
- Black or white sesame seeds.

Method:

1. Wrap the bamboo mat with plastic wrap and place a nori sheet on bamboo mat.
2. Add a handful of prepared sushi rice on the nori mat and spread it over the nori, make the rice covering 1 cm high. Sprinkle with sesame seeds.
3. Flip the nori sheet, so the rice is facing the plastic over the mat. Now you have to place the ingredients on top of nori.
4. On one edge, line up the crab sticks and then avocado.
5. Then roll it inside out and cut into 8 equal pieces.

Shrimp Avocado Sushi Rolls

Ingredients:

- Sushi rice – 2 cups;
- Nori sheets – 2 to 3;
- Sushi grade shrimp – 10;
- Tempura – ½ cup o Avocado – 1;
- Cucumber – 1, long and even;

- Tobiko – 50g;
- BBQ eel – 50g.

Method:

1. In a bowl, mix the tempura with a little bit of water and stir until evenly combined.
2. Add the prepared shrimps in the tempura mixture and deep fry until the outside gets golden brown, about 30 seconds.
3. Spread the rice on the nori sheet, thin flip, so the nori sheet is up. On one edge, lay the cucumber and avocado slices, then lime up shrimps and add eel on top.
4. Roll inside-out and cut the endings.
5. Carefully spread some Tobiko on the roll. Then cut.
6. Serve with soy and teriyaki sauce.

Salmon Nigiri

Ingredients:

- Cooked sushi rice – 2 cups, seasoned;
- Fresh salmon – 10 thin slice;
- Pickled ginger;
- Soy sauce;
- Wasabi.

Method:

1. Wet your fingers with water and shape the seasoned rice into 10 mounds. On each slice of salmon, put a little wasabi and then place them on top of the shaped rice. It will help stick the fish to the rice.
2. Shape with your hands.
3. Serve with pickled ginger and soy sauce on the side.

Spicy Tuna Roll

Ingredients:

- White roasted sesame seeds – 2 tbsp.;
- 2 tsp rice vinegar + ¼ cup water;
- Spicy mayo;
- Sesame oil - ½ tsp.;
- Chopped green onion/scallion – 2 tsp.;
- Sriracha sauce – 3 tsp.;
- Sashimi-grade tuna – 4 ounces, cut into ¼ inch cubes;
- Prepare sushi rice – 1 ½ cups.

Method:

1. In a bowl, combine sesame oil, 1 tsp green onion, sriracha sauce, and tuna.
2. On a bamboo mat, lay a sheet of nori, shiny side down. Wet your fingers with vinegar and water mixture and spread ¾ cup of rice evenly over the nori sheet.
3. Sprinkle the rice with sesame seeds.
4. Flip the nori sheet, so the rice side is facing down. Place half of the tuna mixture at the one end of the nori sheet.
5. Roll the nori into a tight cylinder and cut the roll in slices.
6. Garnish with remaining green onion and add a dollop of spicy mayo on top of each sushi.

Chapter 5 Meat Sushi Recipes

Beef Sushi Rolls

Ingredients:

- Cooked roast beef – 60 oz. cut into long strips;
- Sushi rice – 40 oz., rinsed and drained and cooked;
- Mirin – 2 tbsp.;
- Nori sushi sheets – 2 to 3;
- 2 tbsp. mayonnaise and 2 tsp. wasabi paste mixed;
- Carrot – 1 small, cut into very thin batons;
- Cucumber – ½ small, cut into thin slices;
- Red pepper – ½ small, cut into thin slices.

For the dressing:

- Rice wine vinegar – 4 tbsp.;
- Light soy sauce – 2 tbsp.;
- Sesame oil – ½ tsp.;
- Wasabi paste – ½ tsp.;
- Runny honey – 1 tsp.;
- Prepared pickled ginger – 1 tbsp. finely chopped.

Method:

1. To make the dressing: in a small bowl, mix all the ingredients together and add to a dipping bowl. Set aside.
2. To make the sushi: over the nori sheet (shiny side down), spread an even layer of rice. Keep about 1 cm empty space around the edges. Drizzle with the mirin.
3. Arrange the pepper, cucumber, carrot and beef along the length of the rice. Along the edge of the filling, run a pea-sized blob of wasabi.
4. Slowly roll up the bamboo mat and press lightly to seal.
5. Remove the roll from the mat and keep in a cool place.
6. Cut with a sharp moist knife into 5 to 6 rolls.
7. Serve with the dressing.

Ground Beef Maki Sushi

Ingredients:

- Sushi rice – 300g (prepared with (salt, sugar, rice vinegar, and mirin);
- Ground beef – 100g;
- Ground cumin seeds – 1 tsp.;
- Ground coriander seeds – 1 tsp.;
- Chili powder – ½ tsp.;
- Soy sauce – 1 tbsp.;
- Cucumber – 1 big, sliced into thin long pieces;
- A bowl of rice vinegar;
- Marinated ginger;
- Soy sauce +wasabi;
- Grilled white sesame seeds.

Method:

1. Cook the rice according to package direction. Put the hot rice in a bowl and add the seasoning ingredients. Stir to mix and set aside to cool.
2. In a pan, heat some oil in a frying pan. Add ground beef, soy sauce, chili, cumin, and coriander.
3. Fry until the beef is cooked and set aside to cool.
4. Place a nori sheet on the rolling mat and add cool rice on top.
5. Wet your fingers and spread the rice evenly.
6. Close to the bottom edge, arrange the cucumber and beef on the rice, in a horizontal line.
7. Sprinkle with sesame seeds and roll the nori and gently press each turn.
8. Before doing the last turn, moist the upper edge with rice vinegar.
9. Press gently to roll and set aside.
10. With a sharp knife, cut the sushi in pieces.
11. Serve with marinated ginger, soy sauce, and wasabi.

Beef Sushi

Ingredients:

- Uncooked short-grain white rice – 2 cups;
- Water – 2 cups;
- Cider vinegar – 2 tbsp.;
- Silverbeet – 2 leaves;
- Eggs – 2, well beaten;
- Soy sauce – 2 tbsp. divided;
- Water – 3 tbsp.;
- Vegetable oil – 1 tbsp.;
- Onion – 1, diced;
- Beef stock – 375g, minced;
- Tinned chunk tuna in water – 185g, drained;
- Carrot – 1 julienned;
- Cucumber – 1, julienned;
- Nori – 6 sheets.

Method:

1. Bring 2 cups water and cider vinegar to a boil in a medium saucepan. Add rice and stir. Reduce heat, cover and simmer until rice grains are soft and sticky about 20 minutes.
2. Boil the silverbeet until soft and then cut into strips.
3. Whisk the eggs with 3 tbsp. water and soy sauce. Over medium heat, pour into a medium frypan and cook until thickened. Remove from heat and cut into strips.
4. In a saucepan, heat the vegetable oil over medium-high heat. Add onion and cook until tender. Add 1 tbsp. soy sauce and beef mixture and cook until evenly brown. Drain and set aside.
5. Preheat the oven to 180C.
6. Place the nori sheets on a baking tray and heat in the oven until slightly crisp, about 1 to 2 minutes.
7. Place the nori sheets on the bamboo rolling mat. Arrange rice evenly over the nori sheets.
8. At one edge, line beef, cucumber, tuna, carrot, egg, and silverbeet.
9. The role the sheets tightly and seal with a few sticky rice.
10. Cut into slices and serve.

BBQ Bacon Sushi Rolls:

Ingredients:

- Bacon – 12 slices;
- Ground beef – 500g, minced;
- BBQ rub;
- Emmental-type cheese – 2 sticks;
- BBQ sauce;
- Crumbled nachos;
- Roasted onions;
- Pickled jalapenos.

Method:

1. On the sushi rolling mat, place 6 bacon slices.
2. Season the minced beef with BBQ rub and add a thin layer of meat on the bacon.
3. Add a cheese stick on the meat. Roll up tightly and prepare for the indirect heat.
4. On an indirect zone of the grill, put the Moink-Rolls.
5. Close the lid and at 180C, cook for 35 minutes.

6. After 25 minutes, glaze the Moink-Rolls with BBQ sauce. Then cook for 10 minutes more. Glaze again after 5 minutes.

7. Coat the Moink-Rolls with roasted onions or crumbled nachos and position as desired.

8. Serve the bacon sushi with pickled jalapenos and BBQ sauce.

Beef Roll Sushi

Ingredients:

- Cooked and seasoned sushi rice – 4 cups;
- Cooked beef – 2 cups;
- Avocado – 1, sliced;
- Seasoned black mushrooms;
- Sheet nori – 1 package;
- Eel sauce;
- Gari;
- Soy sauce;

- Wasabi;
- Toasted sesame seeds;
- Seasoned black mushrooms;
- Soy sauce – 1 ½ tbsp.;
- Sugar – 2 tbsp.;
- Soak water from mushrooms – 1 cup;
- Dried Chinese black mushrooms – 4.

Method:

1. Soak dried mushrooms in boiling-hot water for 15 minutes or until soft. Reserve 1 cup of soak water. 2. Rinse the mushrooms and slice.
2. In a small saucepan, place soy sauce, sugar, soak water, and mushrooms. Simmer until almost completely reduced. Let cool.
3. Set down one sheet of nori on a sheet of plastic wrap. Spread rice with wet hands on the top of the nori sheet. Press the rice down, so it sticks.
4. Flip the nori over and place mushrooms, avocado, and beef at the non-rice end.
5. Like a carpet, roll the fillings up from the non-rice end to the nori. Roll tightly.
6. Slice through the plastic wrap with a very sharp wet knife.
7. On top of each piece brush eel sauce and garnish with sesame seeds.
8. Serve with soy sauce and wasabi.

Chapter 6 Dessert Sushi Recipes

Fruit and Coconut Sushi

Ingredients:

- Unsweetened shredded coconut – ½ cup;
- Raw honey – 2 tbsp.;
- Coconut oil – 3 tbsp. divided;
- Splash pure vanilla extract;
- Maple syrup – 1 tbsp.;
- Cocoa powder – 2 tbsp.;
- Fresh fruit;
- Pinch salt.

Method:

1. In a small food processor, place the coconut, vanilla, salt, 1 tbsp. coconut oil, and honey. Blend until combined.
2. Place into a small bowl and keep in the refrigerator.
3. Prepare the fruit filling: cut your choice of fruits into small pieces, and make stacks. Dry them on a paper towel and freeze them, so they stick together.
4. Make the chocolate nori: melt the rest of the 2 tbsp. coconut oil. Combine with a pinch of salt, vanilla extract, maple syrup, and cocoa powder. Mix until smooth and set aside.
5. From a chunk of the chocolate "rice", around one fruit stack. Leave the sides open like regular sushi. Continue with the rest of the fruits stacks and freeze them to set.
6. Once the rolls are set, coat the outside with chocolate "nori." Paint the chocolate around the outside of the rolls with your fingers. Then place in the fridge to set.
7. Serve cold with extra chocolate nori as your soy sauce.

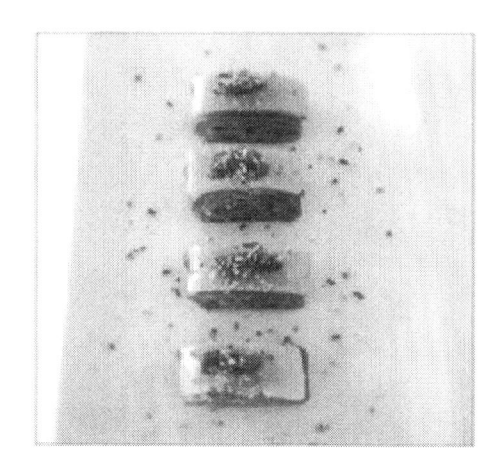

Superfood Dessert Sushi

Ingredients:

- Sushi dough:
- Almond flour – 1 cup;
- Cashews – ½ cup, finely diced;
- Date paste – ¼ cup;
- Vanilla extract – ½ tsp;
- Sea salt – 1/8 tsp.

Berry filling :

- Mixed berries – ¼ cup plus 2 tbsp.;
- Date paste – ½ cup.

Finish:

- Hemp seeds;
- Fruits of choice: strawberry, white peach, mango.

Sushi dough:

1. In a food processor, combine cashews and almond flour and process until finely ground.
2. Add salt, vanilla extract and date paste. Process until mixed well.

Berry filling:

- In the blender, combine berries and date paste. Blend until smooth.

Finish:

- On top of plastic foil, place the sushi dough and cover it with another plastic foil. Roll out the dough with a rolling pin.
- Remove the upper layer of the plastic foil.
- Spread the berry filling on top of the dough.
- Into a dessert sushi roll, roll the dough.
- Cut the roll into smaller sushi pieces
- Garnish with hemp seeds and finely sliced fresh fruit.

Tropical Dessert Sushi

Ingredients:

- Roll wrapper or rice pepper – 3 spring;
- Uncooked sushi rice – 1 cup;
- Light coconut milk – 1 can;
- Cubed pineapple – 2/3 cup;
- Dates – 2/3 cup;
- Unsweetened shred carrot – ¼ cup;
- Macadamia nuts – ¼ cup;
- Sesame seeds – 2 tbsp.;
- Papaya – 2 to 3 slices.

Method:

1. Cook the sushi rice using 2/3 cup water, 1 cup coconut milk, and 1 cup rice. Bring to a boil, cover and cook for 20 minutes or until liquid is absorbed.
2. Combine 2 tbsp. sesame seeds with a handful of macadamia nuts in a food processor and blends to make a flavorful topping.
3. Add 2/3 cup of dates in the food processor and pulse until broken up. Then add the unsweetened coconut and pineapple and blend to mix, but don't puree.
4. With a sharp knife, make very thin papaya slices, about 1 inch wide.
5. On a plastic wrap, place the rice paper or spring roll wrappers. Use warm water to soften the rice paper, then place on your work surface.
6. Add a thin layer of rice on the rice paper, then a long row of date/pineapple filling.
7. Roll tightly and tuck in the ends. Top with a few slices of papaya sashimi.
8. Slice with a sharp knife.
9. Serve sprinkle with sesame/macadamia crumble.

Kiwi, Strawberries and Chocolate Dessert Sushi

Ingredients:

- Jasmine rice – ½ cup;
- Light coconut milk – 1 1/3 cups;
- Granulated sugar – 6 tbsp.;
- Salt – ½ tsp.;
- Butter – 2 tbsp. softened;
- Milk – 1 tbsp.;
- Vanilla extract – ¼ tsp.;
- Cocoa powder – 2 tbsp.;
- All-purpose flour – 5 tbsp.;
- Quartered strawberries – 1 ½ ounces;

- Kiwi – 1 ½ ounces, sliced in long strips Semisweet chocolate chips – 1/3 cup, melted.

Method:

1. In a small saucepan, combine ¼ tsp. salt, 2 tbsp. sugar, coconut milk, and rice. Heat over medium heat, stir and cook until boils. Then lower heat, and simmer until rice is tender and sticky and liquid is absorbed about 20 minutes. Remove from heat and cool to room temperature.
2. Meanwhile, in a medium bowl, mix 4 tbsp. sugar and butter until creamed. Add cocoa powder, vanilla, and milk until smooth. Stir remaining ¼ tsp. salt and flour.
3. Roll the chocolate dough into a 12-inch log and place in the middle of a waxed paper lined large sheet. Cover with a waxed paper and roll the log with a rolling pin into a 12 X6 inch rectangle. Remove the top waxed paper.
4. On top of the chocolate dough, spread room temperature coconut rice. Left ¼ inch border on both sides.
5. Line up the strawberries, then kiwi.
6. Roll the roll in the center and press together firmly.
7. Remove the wax paper and cut into sushi pieces.
8. Add melted chocolate into small soy sauce containers.
9. Serve dessert sushi with chocolate soy sauce.

Marshmallow Dessert Sushi

Ingredients:

- Miniature marshmallows – 10 oz.;
- Challenge butter – ¼ cup, plus more for garnish;
- Rice Krispies cereal – 5 cup;
- Graham cracker crumbs – ¾ cup;
- Marshmallow cream – 7 oz.;
- Hershey's chocolate bars – 6.

Method:

1. Preheat the oven to 200F.

2. With wax paper, line a 10x15 jelly roll pan. Butter the paper and set aside.
3. In a microwave-safe bowl, combine the one-quarter cup of butter and marshmallows. Cover and melt in the microwave on short burst until melts.
4. Stir in graham cracker crumbs and cereals.
5. Press mixture into prepared pan and spread marshmallow cream on top.
6. Then place the chocolate bars on top.
7. Place in the oven for 2 minutes and spread the chocolate with a spatula.
8. Let cool for 10 minutes.
9. Roll the jelly roll and peel away the paper as you roll.
10. Place the roll seam side down and refrigerate until chocolate has set, about 30 to 45 minutes.
11. Slice and serve.

Conclusion

Lastly, here are some video links for you to know more about sushi making:

[Sushi 1](#)

[Sushi 2](#)

[Sushi 3](#)

[Sushi 4](#)

[Sushi 5](#)

Made in the USA
Middletown, DE
22 December 2017